How To Start A Used Car Business

The Ultimate Guide to Dealership Management and Secrets to Buying Low and Selling High

Charles Y. Steele

Copyright ©2024 by Charles Y. Steele

All rights reserved. No part of this work may be reproduced, stored in a retrieval system, or transmitted in any form or by any means, electronic, mechanical, photocopying, recording, or otherwise, without the express prior written permission of the author. To the best of our knowledge and belief, the contents of this e-book are accurate and comprehensive. The author or publisher assumes no liability for any suggestions or recommendations. Both the author and the publisher assume no responsibility for any liability associated with the use of this information.

Table of Contents

INTRODUCTION 5

    Understanding the Used Car Market 9

    Benefits of Starting a Used Car Business 12

Getting Started 15

    Legal Requirements and Licensing 15

    Choosing a Business Structure 19

    Writing a Business Plan 22

    Financing Your Business 25

Location and Facilities 28

    Choosing the Right Location 28

    Lot Layout and Design 31

    Necessary Equipment and Tools 34

Sourcing Inventory 37

    Buying Used Cars at Auctions 37

    Trade-ins and Buying from Private Sellers 40

    Reconditioning Cars for Sale 43

    Managing Inventory Effectively 46

Marketing Your Business 49

- Branding and Identity 49
- Effective Advertising Strategies 52
- Online Presence and Social Media 55
- Networking and Community Engagement 59

Sales Techniques 62
- Understanding Customer Needs 62
- Pricing Strategies 65
- Negotiation Techniques 68
- Closing the Sale 71

Operations Management 74
- Daily Operations and Workflow 74
- Staffing and Employee Management 77
- Customer Service and Satisfaction 80
- Record-Keeping and Administration 83

Legal and Ethical Considerations 86
- Compliance with Automotive Laws 86
- Ethical Selling Practices 89
- Handling Legal Disputes 92

Expanding Your Business 96

- Scaling Up Operations 96
- Diversifying Inventory 100
- Franchising Opportunities 104
- Partnerships and Alliances 107

Challenges and Solutions 110
- Common Pitfalls and How to Avoid Them 110
- Handling Economic Downturns 113
- Competitor Analysis and Market Trends 116

Conclusion 120

INTRODUCTION

John Morrison was a man of ambition, determined to carve out his own piece of the American Dream. After spending years as a sales associate at a bustling new car dealership, John realized that the real opportunity lay in the burgeoning market of used cars. But taking the leap from employee to entrepreneur was daunting—until he found the book that would guide his journey: *How to Start a Used Car Business*.

On a rainy Saturday afternoon, with the scent of coffee filling his small apartment, John turned the first page of the book. It wasn't just any guide; it was a mentor in print, offering not only practical steps but also real insights into the trade he aspired to master.

The book began with an in-depth look at the used car market, providing statistics and trends that immediately hooked John. It wasn't just numbers and graphs; the book painted a picture of the potential for success, framing the used car business as a resilient sector in the economy, less impacted by economic downturns than new car sales. This was exactly the kind of reassurance John needed.

As he delved further, the book covered everything from obtaining the necessary licenses to the intricacies of zoning laws—details that could easily overwhelm a newcomer. Each chapter was meticulously organized, such as Chapter 2: "Getting Started," which walked him through choosing a business structure, writing a business plan, and securing financing—crucial steps for a solid foundation.

John was particularly impressed by the section on sourcing inventory. It described various avenues to acquire cars, from auctions to private sellers, and even touched on the strategies for reconditioning vehicles to maximize profit. The book made clear that success wasn't about selling any car; it was about selling a good car at a fair price.

Marketing was another chapter that stood out. The book emphasized the importance of an online presence and offered up-to-date strategies for digital marketing, essential for competing in today's market. It even included tips on social media advertising, SEO for the dealership's website, and engaging with customers through online platforms.

When John reached the chapters on sales techniques and operations management, he realized the book was more than just a how-to guide—it was a blueprint for running a business. It covered negotiation techniques, pricing strategies, and even how to handle difficult customers, which John found invaluable.

Perhaps most importantly, the book addressed the challenges of the industry. It didn't shy away from the potential pitfalls and how to navigate them, providing solutions and preventive measures to keep the business thriving in the face of obstacles.

Months later, standing on his newly acquired lot filled with a carefully curated selection of used cars, John felt a surge of pride. He had followed the book's advice to the letter, and now, Morrison Motors was open for business.

The grand opening was a hit. As customers browsed the lot, John's confidence soared. He knew he had everything covered—from legal compliance to customer satisfaction—all thanks to the comprehensive guide he had followed.

How to Start a Used Car Business wasn't just a purchase; it was an investment in his future. The book had been instrumental in transforming his dream into reality, providing him with the knowledge and tools needed to succeed.

So why should you buy this book? If you're like John, dreaming of your entrepreneurial venture, this book is your roadmap. It's proof that with the right knowledge and guidance, you can navigate the complexities of the used car industry and steer your way to success. Join the ranks of successful business owners who started with a dream and a book—your journey begins here.

Understanding the Used Car Market

The used car market is a dynamic and significant segment of the automotive industry, offering entrepreneurs a lucrative opportunity to tap into a continuously growing customer base. Unlike new cars, which depreciate rapidly within the first few years, used cars provide a more affordable alternative for consumers, maintaining a steady demand regardless of economic conditions.

To successfully start and operate a used car business, one must first grasp the market's size and structure. This market consists of various channels through which vehicles are sold, including private party sales, used car dealerships, and auction houses. Each channel comes with its own set of advantages and challenges. For instance, purchasing cars from auctions might allow a dealer to acquire inventory at lower prices, but it also involves higher risk as the condition of the vehicles may not be fully known until they are delivered.

Understanding the demographics and purchasing behaviors of potential customers is crucial. Used car buyers range from first-time drivers looking for affordable vehicle options to seasoned car enthusiasts seeking specific models for restoration. By identifying target customer segments, a dealer can tailor their inventory and marketing strategies to meet the specific needs and preferences of their clientele.

Price sensitivity is another important aspect of the used car market. Factors that influence pricing include the make and model of the car, its age, mileage, overall condition, and the current market demand for that type of vehicle. Successful used car dealers develop an adeptness at setting competitive prices that attract buyers while still allowing for a reasonable profit margin.

Economic factors play a significant role in shaping the used car market. During economic downturns, the demand for used cars typically increases as more consumers turn to more budget-friendly options. Conversely, when the economy is strong, consumers might be more inclined to purchase new vehicles. However, recent trends show that even in robust economic times, the allure of a well-maintained, pre-owned vehicle remains strong due to the perceived value and reduced rate of depreciation.

Technological advancements and the growing importance of online sales channels have transformed how used cars are bought and sold. Many consumers now start their car buying journey online, researching different models, comparing prices, and reading reviews before ever stepping foot on a lot. Consequently, a successful used car business must have a strong online presence. This includes maintaining an up-to-date, searchable inventory and possibly offering virtual tours or online financing options to meet the evolving expectations of today's consumers.

The regulatory environment also impacts the used car market. Dealers must comply with a range of laws and regulations, from state-specific requirements regarding vehicle inspections and emissions tests to federal laws concerning lending practices and consumer rights. Keeping abreast of legal changes and ensuring compliance not only protects the business from potential fines and legal issues but also builds trust with customers.

In conclusion, understanding the used car market is foundational for anyone looking to start a used car business. It requires a keen eye for market trends, customer behavior, and regulatory changes, coupled with an ability to adapt to the evolving landscape of automotive sales. Armed with this knowledge, entrepreneurs can better position themselves to capitalize on the opportunities that the used car market presents.

Benefits of Starting a Used Car Business

Starting a used car business offers a range of advantages that can be appealing to aspiring entrepreneurs. One of the primary benefits is the high demand for used cars. As new car prices continue to rise, more consumers are turning to used vehicles as a more affordable option. This shift in consumer behavior ensures a steady stream of customers and potentially high sales volumes for used car dealerships.

Additionally, the initial capital required to start a used car business can be significantly lower than that needed for new car dealerships. Used cars can be acquired at lower costs, especially if purchased at auctions or from private sellers looking to offload their vehicles quickly. This lower startup cost allows entrepreneurs to enter the market more easily and start generating revenue without the burden of excessive loans or investments.

Profit margins in a used car business can also be quite lucrative. By buying cars at a lower price and reconditioning them to sell at a higher value, dealers can maximize their profits. The ability to effectively manage inventory and reconditioning costs directly impacts the profitability of the business. Smart purchasing decisions and efficient operations can result in substantial financial returns.

Another benefit is the flexibility in inventory. Used car dealers have the freedom to stock a variety of makes and models to cater to different customer preferences and budget ranges. This flexibility enables dealers to quickly adapt to market trends and consumer demands, unlike new car dealerships that are typically restricted to specific models and brands based on franchise agreements.

The used car market also offers extensive growth opportunities. Dealers can expand their business by increasing the size of their inventory, diversifying into related areas such as auto parts and repair services, or even opening additional locations. The scalability of the business model is a significant advantage for those looking to build a larger business over time.

Moreover, owning a used car business provides a unique opportunity to tap into the community. Dealers can build strong relationships with local customers and businesses, fostering a loyal customer base through excellent service and community involvement. This local engagement not only helps in building a good reputation but also supports the business through referrals and repeat customers.

Lastly, the used car industry is continually evolving with technological advancements and changes in consumer behavior, providing an exciting environment for entrepreneurs who enjoy dynamic business landscapes. Keeping up with trends like online sales platforms and eco-friendly vehicle preferences can position a dealership as a leader in a competitive market.

In conclusion, starting a used car business offers numerous benefits including lower initial investment, high demand, profitable margins, inventory flexibility, growth opportunities, community involvement, and a dynamic industry environment. These factors make it an attractive option for entrepreneurs looking to enter the automotive industry.

Getting Started

Legal Requirements and Licensing

Navigating the legal requirements and obtaining the necessary licenses is a crucial step in starting a used car business, as it ensures compliance with both local and federal regulations. Each state in the United States has specific requirements, but there are commonalities across the board that potential dealers must understand.

Firstly, acquiring a dealer license is mandatory for anyone looking to sell used cars commercially. This process typically involves submitting an application to the state's Department of Motor Vehicles (DMV) or appropriate regulatory body. The application often requires detailed information about the business, including the physical location, proof of a properly zoned dealership lot, and evidence of a registered business name.

In addition to the dealer license, many states require applicants to provide a surety bond. This bond protects consumers by ensuring that the dealer operates within the state's laws and regulations. The required amount for the bond can vary significantly from one state to another, often depending on the volume of cars the business plans to sell.

Liability insurance is another essential requirement for operating a used car dealership. This insurance protects the business against claims of property damage or personal injury that might occur on the premises or as a result of the operation of any vehicles sold by the dealership. The required coverage amount can vary, so it's important to consult with an insurance agent who understands the automotive industry.

For tax purposes, obtaining a tax identification number from the IRS is necessary. This number is used to collect and remit sales tax on the vehicles sold, if applicable in the state. Some states also require additional specific taxes related to vehicle sales to be managed appropriately.

Local business permits and zoning approvals are also critical. Before a dealership can be established, it's essential to confirm that the chosen location is zoned for automotive sales. Local municipalities may have specific ordinances that regulate signage, parking, and the overall operation of a dealership, which must be adhered to.

Compliance with the Federal Trade Commission (FTC) is also important. The FTC enforces the Used Car Rule, which requires dealers to display a Buyer's Guide in every used car they have for sale. This guide provides important information about the car and spells out the warranty details, helping to ensure transparency and build trust with buyers.

Environmental regulations must also be considered, especially concerning the handling and disposal of fluids and auto parts, which can be hazardous. Compliance with the Occupational Safety and Health Administration (OSHA) regulations is necessary to ensure a safe working environment for all employees.

For ongoing compliance, staying informed about changes in the law is vital. Many dealerships choose to join professional organizations that offer resources, training, and updates on the industry's legal aspects. These organizations can also provide networking opportunities and additional support for new and established dealers.

Meeting these legal requirements and maintaining proper licensing not only protects the business from legal issues but also builds credibility with customers. It demonstrates a commitment to ethical business practices and ensures a foundation that promotes long-term success in the used car industry.

Choosing a Business Structure

Choosing the right business structure is a critical decision when starting a used car business, as it affects everything from legal liability to tax obligations and the ability to raise capital. The most common business structures include sole proprietorship, partnership, limited liability company (LLC), and corporation. Each has its own advantages and considerations that can impact the operation and success of a used car dealership.

A sole proprietorship is the simplest and most straightforward business structure. It is easy to establish and requires fewer formalities, but it does not provide any personal liability protection. This means that personal assets are potentially at risk if the business incurs debt or faces lawsuits. For a used car business, where high-value transactions and significant customer interactions occur, this lack of protection can be a considerable disadvantage.

Partnerships are similar to sole proprietorships but involve two or more people. This structure allows for shared investment and expertise, which can be beneficial in a business that requires a substantial up-front capital investment and diverse skills. However, like sole proprietorships, partnerships generally do not offer personal liability protection. Additionally, partnerships require clear agreements on the division of profit, roles, and responsibilities to prevent conflicts.

A limited liability company (LLC) is a popular choice for many used car dealers because it combines the simplicity of a partnership or sole proprietorship with the liability protection of a corporation. An LLC protects personal assets from business debts and claims. It also offers flexibility in taxation, allowing profits and losses to be passed through to owners' personal income without facing corporate taxes. However, LLCs are subject to more regulations and require more paperwork to establish and maintain than sole proprietorships or partnerships.

Corporations, including C corporations and S corporations, provide the highest level of personal liability protection, separating personal assets from the business's liabilities completely. C corporations allow for potentially unlimited growth through the sale of stock, which can be appealing if significant capital is needed to expand the dealership. However, they are more complex to set up and operate and involve double taxation—once at the corporate level and again on dividends paid to shareholders. S corporations avoid double taxation by allowing income and losses to be passed through to shareholders' personal tax returns, but they face restrictions on the number and type of shareholders they can have.

When selecting a business structure for a used car business, it's essential to consider factors such as the potential risks involved, the financial needs, the tax implications, and the future goals of the dealership. Often, the decision is also influenced by the scale of the operation and the owner's readiness to handle formalities and compliance requirements associated with more complex business structures.

Ultimately, the choice of business structure should support not only the current needs of the used car dealership but also its long-term growth and success. Consulting with legal and financial professionals can provide valuable insights and help tailor the decision to the specific circumstances and goals of the business. Choosing wisely can safeguard the business, facilitate its smooth operation, and optimize its profitability in the competitive used car market.

Writing a Business Plan

Writing a business plan is a critical step in starting a used car business as it lays the foundation for the enterprise's success. A well-constructed business plan serves multiple purposes: it helps clarify the business concept, provides a roadmap for operations, attracts potential investors, and helps secure financing.

The first section of the business plan should detail the business description, including the focus on selling used cars, the types of cars the business will sell, and the target market. This section should also outline the business's unique selling propositions such as competitive pricing, quality service, and a diverse inventory that caters to various customer preferences.

A thorough market analysis follows, which investigates the local demand for used cars, identifies the target customer demographics, and analyzes competitors in the area. This analysis should cover key trends in the used car industry, such as shifts towards more environmentally friendly vehicles or the increasing popularity of online car sales. Understanding these trends and the competitive landscape helps in strategically positioning the business in the market.

The organization and management section of the business plan explains the business structure, whether it's a sole proprietorship, partnership, or corporation, and details about the management team. Including bios and professional backgrounds of the key team members adds credibility and shows expertise in running a used car business.

The sales and marketing strategy is crucial and should clearly describe how the business intends to attract and retain customers. This includes advertising channels that will be used, such as local media, online advertising, and social media platforms. The plan should also detail promotional strategies like discounts, loyalty programs, and after-sales services that will differentiate the business from its competitors.

The operational plan outlines the day-to-day operations of the used car business. This covers the sourcing of cars, inventory management, reconditioning processes, sales processes, and customer service. The operational plan should detail the location of the business, necessary facility improvements, and the types of tools and technology needed to operate efficiently.

Financial projections are critical and must be realistic and detailed. This section includes startup costs like purchasing initial inventory, securing a location, and any necessary renovations or equipment. Ongoing operational costs such as employee salaries, utility expenses, insurance, and marketing should also be included. Revenue projections should be based on market analysis and realistic sales targets. Including break-even analysis, profit and loss forecasts, cash flow statements, and balance sheets will provide a clear financial picture to potential investors and lenders.

Lastly, an appendix can be used to include any additional information that supports the business plan. This might contain credit histories, resumes, product pictures, letters of reference, legal documents, or detailed market studies.

Crafting a detailed and thorough business plan is essential for anyone looking to start a used car business. It not only aids in setting up and organizing the business but also plays a vital role in communicating the business's potential to stakeholders and securing necessary funding.

Financing Your Business

Financing a used car business is a critical step in getting started and requires careful planning and consideration of various funding sources. Most entrepreneurs start by assessing their personal savings to determine how much of their own money they can invest in the business. This initial capital can cover startup costs such as licensing fees, initial inventory acquisition, and leasing a business location.

For those who need additional funding, small business loans from banks or credit unions are a common source. These institutions typically offer loans with competitive interest rates and favorable terms. It is important to have a well-crafted business plan to present to lenders, demonstrating the viability of the business and a clear plan for profitability, which can significantly increase the chances of securing a loan.

Another option is to seek out an SBA loan, which is backed by the Small Business Administration. SBA loans are designed to help small businesses that may not qualify for traditional bank loans. These loans often require less collateral and have lower interest rates, making them attractive for new entrepreneurs. However, the application process can be lengthy and requires thorough documentation.

Equipment financing is particularly relevant for a used car business. This type of financing allows the business to purchase the necessary equipment and inventory without paying the full cost upfront. Payments are made over time, which helps manage cash flow more effectively. This can include loans specifically for purchasing vehicles, which are then paid back as the business earns revenue from sales.

Additionally, lines of credit offer a flexible funding solution. Unlike a traditional loan, which provides a lump sum amount, a line of credit allows a business to draw funds up to a specified limit and pay interest only on the amount borrowed. This can be especially useful for covering unexpected costs or managing seasonal fluctuations in cash flow.

For those looking for more creative financing options, inviting investors into the business can provide the necessary capital while also bringing in additional expertise and networks. Investors may be silent partners or may wish to have a say in the business operations, depending on the agreement. Crowdfunding is another innovative approach, particularly if the business has a unique selling proposition or community focus that can engage potential customers and investors alike.

Leasing vehicles instead of buying them outright can also reduce initial capital requirements. This method allows a business to have a newer and more diverse inventory without the full cost associated with purchasing vehicles. Leasing can improve cash flow and operational flexibility but may result in higher costs over the long term.

Lastly, forging partnerships with other businesses can lead to cost-sharing opportunities. For example, partnering with a local repair shop can reduce overhead costs associated with reconditioning vehicles while also providing a steady stream of business to the partner.

Overall, financing a used car business involves a mix of personal investment, debt, and creative financing strategies. Each option carries its own set of benefits and risks, and the right approach depends on the specific circumstances and goals of the business. Effective financial management from the outset is crucial to ensure the sustainability and growth of the enterprise.

Location and Facilities

Choosing the Right Location

Choosing the right location for a used car business is crucial and can significantly influence its success. The ideal location is easily accessible and visible to potential customers. High traffic areas such as main roads or near intersections where multiple routes converge tend to attract more passersby and can increase spontaneous visits from potential buyers. Visibility from the road is key as it serves as free advertising for the inventory on the lot.

Accessibility is just as important as visibility. Locations near major highways or with easy access from multiple parts of town make it convenient for customers to visit, enhancing customer experience and potentially increasing sales. Additionally, ample parking and easy entry and exit points help create a hassle-free shopping experience for visitors.

The demographic and economic characteristics of the location also play a significant role. Researching local demographics such as average income, age distribution, and consumer behavior can provide insights into what kinds of cars might sell best in that area. For example, a location near urban centers might see higher demand for compact cars or hybrids, while rural areas might have a better market for trucks and SUVs.

Zoning laws are another critical factor to consider. Before finalizing a location, it's important to ensure that the area is zoned for automotive sales. Local zoning regulations may affect various aspects of the business, from the size of signs and the type of business activities allowed to environmental regulations and building codes. Compliance with these regulations is essential to avoid legal issues and penalties.

The size of the lot is another consideration. It should be large enough to not only display a sufficient inventory of cars but also provide space for potential expansion as the business grows. Moreover, facilities for staff and customers, such as a small office and a waiting area, contribute to the professionalism of the business and enhance customer service.

Security is a further consideration when selecting a location. Areas with lower crime rates reduce the risk of vandalism and theft. Installing security systems and good lighting can help protect the inventory and should be considered when evaluating the cost-effectiveness of a location.

Lastly, competition in the area can impact the success of a used car business. Being too close to other used car lots might lead to overly competitive pricing, but being located near new car dealerships can attract customers who are considering both new and used options. Strategic placement relative to competitors can thus leverage consumer traffic and maximize sales opportunities.

In summary, choosing the right location involves a comprehensive analysis of visibility, accessibility, local demographics, zoning laws, facility size, security, and competitive presence. Each of these factors must be carefully balanced to find a location that supports the operational needs of the business and enhances its market potential.

Lot Layout and Design

Effective lot layout and design are crucial components for the success of a used car business. An optimal layout not only maximizes the use of space but also enhances the visibility and accessibility of vehicles, making it easier for customers to browse and select their preferred cars.

When planning the layout, the first consideration is the size of the lot, which should be sufficient to display a diverse inventory without appearing cramped. Strategic placement of cars can create a welcoming environment and guide customers through the lot in a way that naturally showcases featured or high-demand vehicles. For instance, placing newer and more popular models near the front of the lot can attract passersby and draw them into the dealership.

The design of the lot should also take into account the flow of traffic. There should be clear pathways that allow easy movement for both cars and pedestrians. This involves organizing the cars in rows with ample space between them for customers to walk and view the cars from all angles. It is also essential to have designated areas for different types of vehicles, such as SUVs, sedans, and luxury cars, to aid customers in locating their preferred vehicle types quickly.

Parking spaces for customer vehicles are another important aspect of lot design. Convenient and visible customer parking encourages visitors to stop and browse, increasing the likelihood of sales. Additionally, the layout should include a designated area for test drives that allows easy access to the exit and re-entry from the main road, providing a seamless experience for potential buyers.

Lighting is another critical element, particularly if the business operates during the evening or early morning hours. Adequate lighting enhances vehicle visibility and security and creates a safe environment for customers and staff. It also contributes to the aesthetic appeal of the lot, making it look professional and well-maintained.

Signage plays a vital role in lot design as well. Effective signage includes clear markers for different sections of the lot, price tags that are easily readable from a distance, and promotional banners that highlight special deals or popular models. Signage should be strategically placed to be visible from the road to attract passing traffic.

In terms of facilities, a welcoming sales office or showroom can make a significant difference in customer perceptions and sales. The office should be clean, organized, and equipped with comfortable seating, refreshments, and accessible information about the cars and financing options. This space serves as an area for sales discussions and closing deals, so it should reflect the professionalism and values of the dealership.

Finally, the lot should be designed with sustainability in mind. This can include using eco-friendly materials in construction, implementing a rainwater collection system for car washing, and landscaping with native plants to enhance the environmental aesthetics and reduce maintenance costs.

Overall, the layout and design of a used car lot are about creating a functional, customer-friendly environment that maximizes the visibility and appeal of the vehicle inventory, enhances operational efficiency, and makes a positive first impression on visitors. These factors collectively contribute to the business's ability to attract and retain customers, ultimately influencing its success and profitability.

Necessary Equipment and Tools

Starting a used car business requires a variety of equipment and tools to ensure efficient operations and high-quality service. The necessary equipment can be broadly categorized into office equipment, vehicle maintenance tools, and lot maintenance equipment.

Office equipment is essential for the administrative side of the business. This includes computers, software for inventory management, customer relationship management (CRM) systems, and finance tracking. Desks, chairs, and filing systems are also needed to create a functional office space. Additionally, point of sale (POS) systems and secure methods for handling cash and credit card transactions are crucial to streamline sales processes and enhance customer experience.

For vehicle maintenance, a range of tools is required to inspect, repair, and prepare cars for sale. Hydraulic lifts are vital for mechanics to access the undercarriage of vehicles easily. Basic hand tools like wrenches, screwdrivers, and pliers are necessary for various repairs and adjustments. More specialized automotive tools such as OBD (On-Board Diagnostics) scanners are used to diagnose vehicle issues and reset service lights. Air compressors and tire changing machines are also important to manage tire replacements and repairs efficiently.

Detailing equipment is also critical in a used car business to ensure that cars are presentable and appealing to buyers. This includes pressure washers, vacuum cleaners, buffers, and polishing machines. High-quality cleaning supplies like detergents, waxes, polishes, and microfiber cloths help in providing a professional finish to the vehicles.

Lot maintenance equipment is necessary to keep the business premises clean and inviting. This includes landscaping tools like lawnmowers and trimmers for yard maintenance. Snow removal equipment such as snow blowers or plows might be necessary depending on the geographic location of the dealership to keep the lot accessible during winter months. Signage is another important consideration; durable, well-designed signs help to attract passing traffic and guide customers around the lot.

Security is another critical aspect, requiring investment in surveillance cameras and lighting to deter theft and vandalism. A secure, gated area may be necessary for storing vehicles safely, especially after business hours.

For businesses planning to offer financing, additional tools like credit check software might be required to assess the creditworthiness of customers efficiently.

Overall, the right equipment and tools are fundamental for running a successful used car business. They not only facilitate the maintenance and sale of vehicles but also enhance customer service, streamline operations, and protect business assets. Adequate investment in these areas is crucial for maintaining a competitive edge and ensuring long-term profitability.

Sourcing Inventory

Buying Used Cars at Auctions

Buying used cars at auctions is a crucial strategy for sourcing inventory in a used car business, offering numerous advantages including access to a diverse range of vehicles and potentially lower purchase costs. Auctions provide a dynamic setting where dealers can acquire vehicles at competitive prices, which is essential for maintaining profitability.

One of the key aspects of purchasing at auctions is understanding the types of auctions available. There are primarily two kinds: public and dealer-only auctions. Public auctions are open to anyone and often sell cars that are repossessed or have been traded in from private sellers. Dealer-only auctions, which require a dealer license to participate, typically offer a higher quality of cars, such as off-lease vehicles, trade-ins, and fleet cars. These cars tend to be better maintained and can be bought at wholesale prices, which allows dealers to mark them up appropriately for resale.

Successful bidding at auctions requires thorough preparation. Dealers should research vehicles before the auction date, including market values, demand for specific models, and typical repair costs.

Many auction houses provide detailed information about the cars in upcoming lots, often online, allowing dealers to plan their bidding strategy in advance. Some auctions also offer pre-auction viewing days where dealers can inspect cars in person, check for any mechanical issues, and verify vehicle history reports.

Understanding the auction's terms and conditions is crucial. This includes knowledge about buyer's fees, payment policies, and any guarantees or warranties associated with the vehicle. Most auctioned vehicles are sold as-is, which means the buyer assumes all risks once a bid is accepted. This makes the ability to assess a car's condition quickly and accurately a valuable skill.

Participating effectively in auctions also means being prepared financially. Establishing a maximum bid for each vehicle based on its estimated market value and potential repair costs helps avoid overspending. Successful dealers often set strict budgets and adhere to them, ensuring that each purchase has the potential for profit after accounting for refurbishment and administrative costs.

The logistics of attending auctions also need consideration. Auctions might be held at physical locations that require travel or online, which are becoming increasingly popular. Online auctions offer the convenience of participating from anywhere, reducing travel costs and time. However, they also require confidence in bidding without the possibility of an in-depth, pre-bid vehicle inspection.

Finally, building relationships with auction house staff can be beneficial. These relationships can provide inside information about the best lots and potential deals, and facilitate smoother transactions. Regular attendance and consistent participation can also lead to better service and possibly advantageous terms over time.

In conclusion, buying used cars at auctions is an art that combines preparation, knowledge, and strategic bidding. Mastering this aspect of sourcing inventory can significantly enhance the inventory quality and profitability of a used car business. Understanding the intricacies of different types of auctions, preparing thoroughly for bidding, and managing auction logistics effectively are all essential for maximizing the benefits of this sourcing method.

Trade-ins and Buying from Private Sellers

Sourcing inventory is a critical aspect of running a successful used car business, and two of the most effective methods are accepting trade-ins and buying directly from private sellers. These approaches offer distinct advantages that can help maintain a diverse and profitable inventory.

Trade-ins are a key strategy for used car dealerships as they provide a dual benefit. Firstly, they help facilitate new sales by allowing customers to offset the cost of their new purchase with their old vehicle. This makes purchasing more accessible and attractive to potential buyers, potentially increasing the dealership's sales volume. Secondly, trade-ins supply the dealership with a steady stream of inventory. These vehicles can often be acquired below market value, especially if they are traded for new cars, which can lead to higher profit margins once they are reconditioned and sold.

Handling trade-ins requires a systematic approach to assess each vehicle's value accurately. Dealers need to be skilled in appraisal, understanding market trends, and the condition of the vehicle to offer a fair price that maximizes profitability while also appealing to the customer. Efficient processing and reconditioning of these vehicles are crucial to quickly turning them around for resale, which helps keep inventory fresh and finances fluid.

Buying cars from private sellers is another strategic approach to sourcing inventory. This method often allows dealers to purchase vehicles at a lower cost than buying from auctions or through trade-ins. Private sellers are typically looking to sell quickly and may not be aware of the true market value of their car, which can be leveraged by knowledgeable dealers to buy inventory at competitive prices.

Engaging with private sellers requires effective marketing and communication skills. Dealers must establish a trustworthy presence in the community and online to attract private sellers. Utilizing platforms such as social media, local classifieds, and online marketplaces can significantly increase the dealership's visibility to potential sellers. Building a reputation for fair deals, quick processing, and good customer service encourages private sellers to choose a dealership over other selling options like private buyer transactions or other dealers.

However, purchasing from private sellers also presents challenges such as a higher risk of acquiring vehicles with hidden problems or unclear histories. To mitigate these risks, it's crucial to perform thorough inspections and history checks before purchasing. Establishing a network of trusted mechanics and utilizing vehicle history report services can aid in assessing the true condition and value of a car.

Both trade-ins and purchasing from private sellers require strong negotiation skills to secure inventory at prices that leave room for profit after any necessary repairs and reconditioning. Negotiation also plays a role in maintaining good relationships with sellers, which can lead to repeat business and referrals, further expanding the dealership's sourcing network.

By effectively managing trade-ins and acquisitions from private sellers, dealers can maintain a diverse and desirable inventory, driving sales and profitability. Each method requires distinct skills and strategies, but together, they form a comprehensive approach to inventory sourcing that can sustain a used car business through various market conditions.

Reconditioning Cars for Sale

Reconditioning cars for sale is a critical step in the process of running a successful used car business. This phase involves taking previously owned vehicles that have been sourced from auctions, trade-ins, or private sellers, and preparing them to meet customer expectations and safety standards. Effective reconditioning not only enhances the appeal of the cars but also increases their market value, helping to secure a better profit margin.

The reconditioning process begins with a thorough assessment of each vehicle. This includes a detailed inspection of the car's mechanical condition, bodywork, interior, and features. Mechanics check for engine problems, transmission issues, and other major systems to ensure they function properly. This might involve diagnostic tests to uncover any hidden issues that could affect performance or safety.

After the assessment, necessary repairs are carried out. This can range from simple fixes like replacing worn brake pads or tires to more extensive repairs such as overhauling the transmission or fixing significant engine problems. Ensuring that major mechanical components are in good working order is crucial, as it directly impacts the reliability and drivability of the vehicle.

Cosmetic improvements are also a significant part of reconditioning. This includes repairing dents and scratches, a fresh paint job if necessary, and fixing or replacing damaged trim or fixtures. The goal is to make the car look as appealing as possible. Interior reconditioning might involve deep cleaning, repairing or replacing upholstery, fixing broken knobs or features, and ensuring that all electronic components work correctly.

It's also important to address any safety issues. This includes making sure that all safety features such as airbags, brakes, seatbelts, and lights are fully operational. Safety checks are not only essential for the future driver's safety but also play a crucial role in the dealership's reputation and legal compliance.

Detailing the car is the final step in the reconditioning process. This involves deep cleaning both the interior and exterior to a standard that enhances its showroom appeal. Professional detailing can transform the look of a car, making it more attractive to potential buyers. Detailing tasks typically include shampooing carpets, conditioning leather seats, cleaning vents, polishing the exterior, and ensuring that the vehicle is odor-free.

Efficiently managing the reconditioning process requires a good system for tracking costs and progress on each vehicle. Keeping costs under control is vital, as overspending on reconditioning can erode the profit margin that the dealership stands to make on the sale of the vehicle. Dealers must balance the cost of reconditioning with the expected sale price to ensure profitability.

In summary, reconditioning cars for sale involves a comprehensive approach that includes mechanical repairs, cosmetic improvements, safety checks, and detailing. Each of these components is crucial in preparing a used vehicle for sale, ensuring it meets customer expectations, adheres to safety standards, and achieves a desirable market value. Effective reconditioning not only contributes to customer satisfaction but also enhances the dealership's reputation and profitability.

Managing Inventory Effectively

Managing inventory effectively is crucial for the success of a used car business. The process begins with sourcing inventory, which requires a keen understanding of the market and strategic purchasing decisions. A primary source for acquiring used cars is through auctions, which include both online and physical auction houses. These venues often offer a diverse range of vehicles at varying price points, allowing dealers to purchase cars that meet specific customer demands and budgetary constraints.

Trade-ins are another significant source of inventory. By accepting customers' old vehicles as part of the payment for a new purchase, dealers can refresh their stock while providing value to buyers. This method not only helps in acquiring inventory at a potentially lower cost but also encourages new sales by reducing the upfront financial burden on customers.

Purchasing cars from private sellers provides an additional avenue for inventory acquisition. These transactions may offer the opportunity to negotiate better deals, especially if the seller is motivated to sell quickly due to personal circumstances. However, it requires diligence in inspection and verification to ensure that the vehicles meet quality standards.

Once the cars are acquired, it is essential to conduct a thorough assessment of each vehicle. This evaluation should include a detailed inspection and necessary repairs to ensure that cars are in sellable condition. Reconditioning not only improves the vehicle's appeal but also increases its market value, enhancing profit margins.

Effective inventory management also involves pricing strategies that reflect the current market conditions and the cost of acquisition and reconditioning. Dynamic pricing can be used to adjust prices based on inventory age, market demand, and seasonal trends. This strategy helps in accelerating the turnover rate and reducing the holding costs associated with unsold inventory.

Inventory tracking is another critical aspect. Utilizing inventory management software can help in monitoring stock levels, managing reconditioning tasks, and tracking sales performance. This technology enables dealers to make informed decisions about when to reduce prices or increase promotional efforts to move stagnant inventory.

Moreover, maintaining a balanced inventory is key. It involves having a diverse selection of vehicles that cater to different tastes and budgets. This diversity ensures that the dealership can attract a wider range of customers and meet various consumer needs, from economical compact cars to luxury vehicles.

Lastly, forecasting future trends and consumer preferences is vital in managing inventory effectively. Staying informed about industry developments, such as the rising popularity of electric vehicles or shifts in consumer buying patterns, allows dealers to adapt their inventory accordingly. By anticipating market trends, dealers can proactively source vehicles that are likely to be in high demand, positioning their business for continued success.

In summary, managing inventory effectively in a used car business involves strategic sourcing, diligent vehicle assessment, dynamic pricing strategies, advanced inventory tracking, maintaining a diverse stock, and forecasting market trends. These practices ensure that the dealership remains competitive, profitable, and aligned with consumer demands and industry developments.

Marketing Your Business

Branding and Identity

Branding and identity are crucial components of marketing a used car business as they significantly influence how customers perceive and interact with your dealership. Effective branding involves creating a distinctive image and reputation that resonates with potential buyers, setting your business apart from competitors. This starts with a memorable name and a professional logo that reflect the quality and reliability of the cars you sell. These elements should be consistent across all marketing materials, from business cards to your website, ensuring they communicate the same message and visual style.

Developing a strong brand identity also involves defining your unique selling proposition (USP) which highlights what makes your dealership different. Whether it's offering competitive prices, exceptional customer service, a specialized selection of vehicles, or comprehensive post-purchase support, your USP should address specific customer needs and desires that competitors may overlook. This aspect of branding helps to build a narrative around your business that attracts and retains customers.

Your dealership's reputation is another pivotal element of its identity. Encouraging satisfied customers to leave positive reviews online and share their experiences through word of mouth can bolster your dealership's image as trustworthy and customer-focused. Responding professionally to any negative feedback demonstrates your commitment to customer satisfaction and can actually enhance your reputation if handled correctly.

In addition, your brand identity should be integrated into all aspects of your marketing strategy. This includes advertising campaigns, promotional materials, and your digital presence. Utilizing social media effectively allows you to reinforce your brand identity by engaging directly with customers, showcasing your inventory, and sharing customer testimonials and stories. These platforms offer a dynamic way to maintain visibility and enhance the dealership's personality, making it more relatable and accessible to a broader audience.

Visual elements are also significant in branding your business. The design of your website, the layout of your car lot, the style of your advertisements, and even the uniforms of your staff should all reflect your brand's personality and values. Consistency in these areas ensures that customers have a cohesive and positive experience at every touchpoint, further strengthening your brand identity.

Finally, community involvement can significantly enhance your dealership's brand identity. Participating in local events, sponsoring local sports teams, or engaging in charity activities can position your dealership as an integral part of the local community. This not only increases brand visibility but also establishes your business as a responsible and caring organization, which can be a powerful differentiator in the marketplace.

Overall, effective branding and identity for a used car business mean more than just a logo or a catchy slogan—it's about creating a comprehensive image that conveys trust, quality, and commitment to service at every opportunity. This approach not only attracts more customers but also builds a loyal customer base that is crucial for long-term success.

Effective Advertising Strategies

Effective advertising strategies are crucial for the success of a used car business, as they help attract potential buyers and convert them into loyal customers. One of the foundational approaches is developing a strong brand identity, which resonates with the target market. This can be achieved by creating a memorable logo, a catchy slogan, and a consistent theme across all advertising materials that reflect the quality and reliability of the cars being sold.

Digital marketing is paramount in today's market. An optimized website serves as the central hub for your business, providing essential information such as inventory, prices, and contact details. Search engine optimization (SEO) techniques should be employed to ensure the website ranks highly in search results when potential customers search for used cars in your area. Additionally, pay-per-click (PPC) advertising can drive targeted traffic to your website, with ads placed on search engines and other relevant sites.

Social media platforms offer powerful tools for engaging with customers and promoting your inventory. Regular posts featuring new arrivals, special deals, and customer testimonials can keep the audience engaged. Platforms like Facebook and Instagram also offer advanced targeting options for ads, allowing you to reach specific demographics likely to purchase a used car.

Email marketing remains an effective method to keep in touch with past customers and nurture leads. By sending newsletters, promotions, and updates about new stock or services, you can keep your dealership top of mind. Ensuring that your email content is both informative and engaging will help increase open and click-through rates.

Community engagement is another strategic way to advertise your business locally. Participating in local events, sponsoring sports teams, or hosting your own community events can increase your visibility and reputation within the community. These activities not only advertise your business but also build trust and loyalty among local consumers.

Offline advertising methods such as billboards, local newspapers, and radio ads continue to be effective, especially in areas with less internet penetration or where traditional media is still widely consumed. These methods help in building brand recognition and can direct potential customers to your online platforms for more information.

Finally, developing partnerships with local businesses such as repair shops, auto part stores, and service centers can help cross-promote services. For instance, offering a discount or referral fee to partners who send buyers your way can extend your reach and bring in customers who might not have been reached through traditional or digital advertising alone.

By combining these strategies, a used car business can create a comprehensive advertising plan that not only reaches a wide audience but also effectively converts interest into sales. The key is to maintain consistency in messaging across all platforms and to adjust strategies based on what works best in engaging potential customers and driving traffic to your dealership.

Online Presence and Social Media

In today's digital age, establishing an online presence and utilizing social media are critical components of marketing a used car business. A robust online presence ensures that potential customers find your dealership when they search for used cars online. This presence typically begins with a professionally designed website that serves as the digital face of your business. A good website not only showcases your inventory with high-quality photos and detailed information about each vehicle but also includes contact information, directions to your dealership, and an about section that conveys your business's values and commitment to customer service. Incorporating SEO (Search Engine Optimization) strategies is essential to increase the visibility of your website in search engine results, making it easier for potential customers to find you.

Social media platforms like Facebook, Instagram, and Twitter offer additional avenues to connect with customers. By regularly posting engaging content such as featured vehicles, special promotions, and customer testimonials, you can keep your audience interested and engaged. Social media also provides a platform for real-time interaction with customers, where you can respond to inquiries, participate in conversations, and build relationships that encourage trust and loyalty. Additionally, these platforms allow for targeted advertising, which can be customized based on geographic location, demographics, and interests to reach potential buyers more effectively.

Moreover, video marketing has become an invaluable tool in the digital marketing landscape. Platforms such as YouTube offer a way to provide virtual tours of vehicles, showcase the features and conditions of the cars, and share video testimonials from satisfied customers. These videos can then be embedded on your website or shared across social media platforms, providing a dynamic way to engage customers and give them a closer look at what you offer.

Email marketing also plays a pivotal role in nurturing leads and maintaining customer relationships. By collecting email addresses through your website and at your dealership, you can send out newsletters, special offers, and personalized communications to keep your dealership top of mind. Well-crafted emails can drive traffic to your website, promote current inventory, and increase repeat business by reminding previous customers of services such as maintenance or special deals on new arrivals.

To track the effectiveness of your online marketing efforts, tools like Google Analytics can monitor your website's traffic and provide insights into visitor behavior and preferences. Social media analytics tools offered by various platforms can also track engagement rates, post reach, and the effectiveness of paid advertising campaigns. This data is invaluable for refining your marketing strategies and ensuring you invest in the most effective tactics for reaching and engaging your target audience.

Finally, online reviews and ratings are influential factors for consumers in the automotive market. Encouraging satisfied customers to leave positive reviews on platforms like Google, Yelp, and your Facebook page can enhance your dealership's reputation and trustworthiness. Monitoring these reviews and responding to feedback, both positive and negative, demonstrates your commitment to customer satisfaction and can sway potential customers in your favor.

Through these digital channels, a used car business can expand its reach, build a robust brand identity, and drive sales more effectively than through traditional marketing methods alone. The key is to maintain a consistent and professional online presence that aligns with the overall goals and values of your business, thereby attracting and retaining customers in a competitive market.

Networking and Community Engagement

Networking and community engagement are crucial components of marketing a used car business. These strategies not only increase visibility but also build trust and credibility within the local area, which are vital for attracting and retaining customers. By actively participating in local events, joining business associations, and partnering with other local businesses, a used car dealership can establish a strong presence in the community.

Building a robust network through local chambers of commerce and business groups provides multiple opportunities for a used car business. These groups often host events, workshops, and meetings where business owners can connect, share insights, and collaborate on promotions. These interactions can lead to strategic partnerships, where businesses jointly market their services, thereby reducing individual marketing costs and reaching wider audiences.

Engaging with the community also involves participating in local events such as fairs, charity drives, or sponsorships of sports teams. Such engagement demonstrates the business's commitment to the community's welfare and can significantly enhance its reputation.

This involvement helps personalize the business, making it more relatable and approachable to potential customers.

Social media platforms are also powerful tools for networking and community engagement. Creating a business page on platforms like Facebook, Instagram, and Twitter allows a dealership to connect with the community in a more informal and interactive way. Posts about new arrivals, special deals, customer testimonials, and behind-the-scenes content can engage audiences and drive traffic to the dealership. These platforms also provide an excellent avenue for receiving and responding to customer feedback, which can improve service and increase customer satisfaction.

Email newsletters are another effective way to keep in touch with customers and local contacts. Regular updates about the business, the local community, and the automotive industry can keep the audience engaged and informed. This constant contact keeps the dealership at the forefront of customers' minds when they consider purchasing a vehicle.

Additionally, hosting or participating in car-related events such as car shows, auto workshops, or driving courses can attract car enthusiasts and potential buyers. These events can serve as both a marketing tool and a platform for demonstrating expertise in the automotive field, which can attract customers looking for knowledgeable and reliable dealers.

In conclusion, effectively networking and engaging with the community are indispensable strategies for marketing a used car business. These efforts not only boost the business's visibility and reputation but also foster relationships with potential and existing customers, creating a loyal customer base that is crucial for long-term success.

Sales Techniques

Understanding Customer Needs

Understanding customer needs is a fundamental aspect of any successful used car business. This involves more than just knowing which cars are in demand; it requires a deep understanding of the motivations, financial constraints, and personal preferences of potential buyers. Salespeople must develop the ability to listen actively and empathize with customers to truly grasp what they are looking for in a vehicle.

The process starts with effective communication. Salespeople should ask open-ended questions that encourage customers to express their needs and desires for their next car. Questions about what the customer liked or disliked about their previous vehicle, how they plan to use the new car, and what their budget looks like are all crucial. This not only helps in identifying the right vehicle for them but also builds a relationship of trust and understanding.

Another key element is being aware of the broader market trends and how they influence individual buyers. For instance, if there is a rising trend in fuel-efficient cars, salespeople should be ready to highlight the fuel efficiency of vehicles in their lot. Understanding broader trends can also help in inventory management, ensuring that the dealership stocks cars that align with current customer preferences.

Sales techniques must also adapt to different types of buyers. Some customers may be very price-sensitive, looking for the best deal possible, while others might prioritize features or the model year. Salespeople need to identify these priorities quickly and adjust their sales pitch accordingly. For price-sensitive customers, explaining financing options or showing how a particular car is priced competitively might be effective. For those interested in features, a detailed demonstration of the car's technology and comforts could be more persuasive.

Empathy plays a critical role in understanding customer needs. By putting themselves in the customers' shoes, salespeople can better appreciate the factors that drive their decisions. This empathy can lead to more personalized interactions, which are likely to result in higher customer satisfaction and increased sales.

Customer feedback is also invaluable. Encouraging customers to provide feedback after their purchase or even after a simple sales interaction can provide insights into what the dealership is doing right and what needs improvement. This feedback can be a direct guide to refining sales strategies and customer service approaches.

Training and continuous learning are essential for sales teams. Regular training sessions that focus on new sales techniques, customer service skills, and understanding the latest automotive trends can equip salespeople with the tools they need to successfully meet customer needs.

Finally, leveraging technology can enhance understanding of customer needs. Tools like CRM systems can track customer interactions and preferences, providing salespeople with valuable information before they even initiate contact with a potential buyer. This information can tailor the sales approach to meet the specific needs and interests of each customer.

In sum, understanding customer needs in the used car business is about creating a customer-centric sales approach that utilizes active listening, empathy, market awareness, and technological tools. By focusing on these areas, dealerships can improve their customer relationships, increase sales, and build a strong, loyal customer base.

Pricing Strategies

Pricing strategies in the used car business are critical for maximizing profitability while remaining competitive in the market. Effective pricing requires a deep understanding of both the local market conditions and the broader trends in the automotive industry. One of the first steps in developing a pricing strategy is thorough market research. This involves analyzing the prices of similar vehicles in the area, understanding the demographics of potential buyers, and identifying what special features or conditions, such as mileage, make, and model year, influence the selling price of a vehicle.

Dynamic pricing is a popular strategy used by successful used car dealerships. This approach allows prices to be adjusted based on real-time market data and inventory levels. For example, if a particular model is in high demand but low supply, its price can be increased to capitalize on market conditions. Conversely, if a car has been in inventory for an extended period, its price might be lowered to facilitate a quicker sale.

Cost-plus pricing is another strategy, where a fixed markup is added to the cost of acquiring and reconditioning the vehicle. This method is straightforward and ensures that each car sold generates a minimum profit margin. However, it might not always align with market dynamics, which can lead to overpricing or underpricing of vehicles.

Psychological pricing can also be effective in the used car market. Setting prices just below a round number, such as $9,995 instead of $10,000, can make a price appear significantly lower in the eyes of consumers, thereby increasing the attractiveness of the deal. This strategy leverages consumer psychology to boost sales and can be particularly effective when combined with promotions or special deals.

Value-based pricing is particularly suited to the used car business because it focuses on the perceived value of the vehicle to the customer rather than just the cost incurred to put the car on the lot. This strategy considers the vehicle's brand, reputation, condition, and rare features that might not be available on other similar models currently available. This requires a keen understanding of what drives value for customers in your specific market segment.

Another aspect of pricing strategy in the used car business involves transparency and trust-building with customers. Many successful dealerships are now offering no-haggle pricing, where the price on the vehicle is the selling price, eliminating potentially stressful negotiations. This straightforward pricing can enhance the customer experience and build trust, leading to higher customer satisfaction and increased repeat and referral business.

Promotional pricing strategies such as time-sensitive discounts or bundling services like free oil changes for a year with a purchase can also be effective in boosting sales. These strategies create a sense of urgency and add value for the customer, making it more likely they will commit to a purchase.

Finally, monitoring and continuously refining pricing strategies is essential. This might involve utilizing software tools that track market trends and inventory levels, allowing dealers to adjust prices swiftly and effectively. Regular reviews of sales performance and profitability also help ensure that the pricing strategy remains aligned with business goals and market conditions.

By implementing a thoughtful and flexible pricing strategy, used car businesses can attract and retain customers, maximize profits, and stand out in a competitive market.

Negotiation Techniques

Effective negotiation techniques are critical in the used car business, as they directly influence the profitability of each transaction and the satisfaction of every customer. Successful negotiators in the used car industry understand that preparation is key. This includes knowing the vehicle's market value, its condition, and any repairs or modifications that have been made. Salespeople should also be familiar with their inventory's history, including acquisition costs, to ensure negotiations are grounded in realistic financial parameters.

Building rapport with customers is another fundamental aspect of negotiation. Salespeople should strive to create a friendly and professional atmosphere, which can make negotiations smoother and more productive. Listening actively to customer needs and concerns not only helps in tailoring the sales approach but also in establishing trust and respect, essential components in any negotiation.

Transparency is vital in used car negotiations. Providing customers with clear information about the car's condition, including any faults or issues, can prevent misunderstandings and foster trust. Transparent negotiations are likely to result in deals that satisfy both parties, reducing the chances of post-sale complaints or negative reviews.

Another effective technique is the strategic use of silence. After making an offer or presenting a price, giving the customer time to think without pressure can often lead to a favorable outcome. This silence allows the customer to consider the offer and can indicate that the salesperson is confident in the value of the vehicle and the fairness of the price.

It's also important to understand the art of concession-making. Skilled negotiators know which aspects of the deal they can be flexible on, such as price, warranty extensions, or additional services like free oil changes or tire rotations. Offering these concessions can make a customer feel valued and more likely to agree to the deal. However, it's crucial that any concessions are made strategically, ensuring the profitability of the deal isn't compromised.

Understanding and adapting to different customer types and their buying behaviors is another essential negotiation skill. Some customers are focused solely on price, while others might value reliability or vehicle specifications more. Tailoring the negotiation strategy to meet the specific needs and priorities of the customer can increase the chances of closing a sale.

Using positive language throughout the negotiation process can also influence the outcome favorably. For example, focusing on what can be done, such as adjusting the payment terms, rather than what cannot be done, such as changing the car's mileage, helps maintain a constructive atmosphere.

Finally, knowing when to close the deal is as important as how the negotiation is conducted. Recognizing buying signals from the customer, such as agreeing with the terms, nodding affirmatively, or discussing next steps like insurance or registration, can indicate that it's time to finalize the deal. Effective closers ensure all terms are clear and that every promise made during the negotiation is documented and honored.

Incorporating these negotiation techniques can significantly enhance the success of a used car business, leading to higher sales, greater customer satisfaction, and ultimately, a stronger reputation in the market.

Closing the Sale

Closing the sale in a used car business is both an art and a science, demanding a nuanced understanding of sales techniques tailored to individual customers while maintaining efficiency across transactions. The first step towards effective closing is building rapport with potential buyers. Trust and comfort are crucial, as they can significantly influence a buyer's decision-making process. Salespersons should engage in genuine conversations, listen actively to understand the customers' needs and preferences, and demonstrate thorough knowledge about the vehicles on the lot.

Understanding customer needs is pivotal. A successful salesperson can align what's available on the lot with a customer's desires and budget constraints. This might involve asking targeted questions that help identify what the customer values most in a vehicle, whether it's fuel efficiency, safety features, or perhaps the make and model. From there, presenting vehicles that meet these criteria without showing too many alternatives helps to avoid overwhelming the customer with choices, a tactic known as choice paralysis.

Demonstrating the value of a vehicle encompasses not just pointing out its features but also relating them to the benefits they bring to the customer. This might involve explaining how a car's advanced braking system offers safety for a family or how its fuel efficiency can reduce daily commuting costs. Such tailored conversations can make the vehicle more appealing and show that the salesperson understands the buyer's needs.

Pricing strategies are integral to closing the sale. Transparent pricing, where all costs are clearly explained, helps in building trust. Offering flexible payment options like financing can also make the purchase more attainable and appealing. Furthermore, knowing when to offer a discount and how to frame it can be the nudge a hesitant buyer needs to make a decision. Discounts should be presented as limited-time offers to create a sense of urgency.

Negotiation is another critical element in closing sales. It requires a balance between being firm and accommodating. A good negotiator remains open to customer concerns and preferences but also guides the conversation towards a mutually beneficial agreement. Training in negotiation techniques is invaluable, helping salespersons maintain profitability while satisfying customer needs.

Trial closes are useful techniques throughout the sales process. Phrases like "How does this sound to you?" or "Would this meet your needs?" help gauge a customer's readiness to buy and identify any remaining objections that need to be addressed before they are ready to commit.

Finally, assuming the sale can be a powerful psychological tool. By discussing next steps as though the customer has already decided to purchase, such as talking about financing applications or vehicle delivery arrangements, the salesperson can subtly lead the customer towards finalizing the deal.

Effective closing techniques in the used car business are not just about making a sale but ensuring the customer leaves satisfied and likely to return or refer others. By focusing on building relationships, understanding customer needs, and applying strategic negotiation and pricing tactics, a used car salesperson can significantly increase their success rate in closing sales. This not only drives revenue but also enhances the dealership's reputation, contributing to long-term success in the competitive used car market.

Operations Management

Daily Operations and Workflow

Effective daily operations and workflow are critical for the success of a used car business. To manage operations efficiently, the day starts with a review of the inventory to ensure that all vehicles are accounted for and properly displayed on the lot. This is complemented by regular maintenance checks to keep each car in optimal selling condition, such as cleaning, checking fluid levels, and ensuring the batteries are charged.

Staff meetings are an essential part of the morning routine. These gatherings are used to brief team members on the day's goals, discuss any customer appointments, and address potential issues with inventory or paperwork. This keeps everyone informed and aligned with the business objectives for the day.

Customer interactions form a significant part of daily activities. Employees should be trained to handle various customer service scenarios, from initial inquiries and test drives to negotiations and sales closings. Each interaction should be logged in a customer relationship management (CRM) system to track leads, follow up on potential sales, and maintain customer relationships.

Paperwork is a constant in the used car business and must be managed meticulously. This includes processing titles, registration documents, and financing agreements. Employees responsible for this aspect must ensure compliance with all local and state regulations to avoid legal complications.

Marketing activities also need to be part of the daily workflow. This could involve updating the dealership's website, posting on social media platforms, and responding to online inquiries. Effective online engagement can drive foot traffic to the dealership and increase sales opportunities.

Inventory acquisition is another ongoing operation. This includes attending auctions, evaluating trade-ins, and purchasing from private sellers. Keeping the inventory fresh and aligned with market demands requires constant attention and quick decision-making to capitalize on good deals.

The end of the day involves a wrap-up session where sales and customer interactions are reviewed. This is also a time to plan for the next day, including setting up test drives, arranging vehicle repairs or detailing, and any other customer follow-ups.

Regular training and development sessions are crucial to keep staff updated on the latest sales techniques, customer service skills, and industry regulations. Investing in employee growth not only improves business operations but also boosts staff morale and retention.

Effective operations management in a used car business is about creating a structured environment where tasks are performed efficiently and consistently. By maintaining a clear focus on daily operations and workflow, a dealership can provide excellent customer service, manage its inventory effectively, and ensure compliance with all regulatory requirements, thereby setting the stage for sustained business success.

Staffing and Employee Management

Effective staffing and employee management are crucial for the success of any used car business. Employing the right people and managing them efficiently can significantly enhance both customer satisfaction and operational efficiency. When starting a used car business, the first step in staffing is to determine the roles that need filling. Typical positions might include salespeople, finance officers, service technicians, and administrative personnel. Each role requires specific skills and attributes; for example, sales staff need excellent communication and negotiation skills, while technicians require a strong technical background in vehicle maintenance and repair.

Once the necessary roles are identified, the recruitment process can begin. This process should focus on attracting candidates who not only have the required professional qualifications but also fit the company's culture and values. Utilizing online job portals, local community boards, and industry-specific recruitment agencies can help cast a wide net to find the best candidates. Additionally, offering competitive salaries, benefits, and opportunities for professional development can attract higher-quality applicants.

After hiring, the focus shifts to training and development. Even experienced hires need to understand the specific processes and expectations of their new employer. Effective training programs cover not only technical skills but also customer service and sales techniques, ensuring that all employees are equipped to contribute to the business's success right from the start. Regular training sessions can also be beneficial, keeping staff updated on new industry trends, technological tools, and changes in regulations.

Performance management is another key aspect of employee management. This involves setting clear performance goals, providing regular feedback, and conducting formal evaluations. Goals should be realistic, aligned with the business objectives, and communicated clearly to each employee. Feedback should be constructive, aiming to motivate employees and address any areas needing improvement. Formal evaluations, conducted annually or semi-annually, help review an employee's overall performance, discuss future goals, and potentially revise compensation and benefits.

Motivation and employee retention are also vital. Employees who feel valued and fairly treated are more likely to stay with the company long-term, reducing turnover costs and building a more experienced team. Strategies to improve employee satisfaction include recognizing and rewarding good performance, creating a positive and inclusive work environment, and offering paths for career advancement.

Finally, compliance with labor laws and regulations is essential in managing staff. This includes understanding and implementing standards related to wages, hours, discrimination, and workplace safety. Failure to comply can result in legal issues and significant penalties, which can harm the business's finances and reputation.

By prioritizing effective staffing and employee management, a used car business can build a dedicated, skilled team that drives sales, enhances customer satisfaction, and maintains smooth operations. This, in turn, solidifies the foundation for sustainable business growth and profitability.

Customer Service and Satisfaction

In the used car business, customer service and satisfaction are pivotal for success. Providing excellent customer service begins with transparency and honesty in every transaction. This approach not only builds trust but also fosters a positive reputation for the dealership. Customers are more likely to recommend a business where they felt valued and fairly treated, which can lead to increased repeat and referral business.

Effective communication is another crucial aspect of customer service. Staff should be trained to listen actively to customer needs and concerns, providing clear and concise information about the vehicles and services offered. This includes discussing car history, condition, and pricing openly, which helps in making customers feel informed and secure in their purchasing decisions.

The responsiveness of the business also plays a significant role in customer satisfaction. Quick responses to inquiries and concerns show that the business values its customers and their time. Whether it's a response to a phone call, email, or a query on the lot, prompt attention can make the difference between a sale and a missed opportunity.

After-sales service is equally important in maintaining customer satisfaction. Offering warranties, return policies, and follow-up services can reassure customers of their purchase and enhance their overall experience. Follow-up calls or emails to ensure that the customer is satisfied with their purchase or to address any post-sale issues can further demonstrate commitment to customer service.

Training staff to handle complaints and resolve disputes effectively is essential. Even with the best practices in place, issues can arise, and the ability to handle these situations professionally can prevent damage to the business's reputation. Empowering employees with the skills to resolve conflicts can turn potentially negative experiences into positive ones, improving customer retention.

Creating a customer-centric culture within the dealership encourages staff to prioritize customer needs and satisfaction continually. This culture can be fostered through regular training, incentives for excellent customer service, and by leadership setting examples in customer interactions.

Personalization can also enhance customer satisfaction. Recognizing returning customers, remembering their preferences, and tailoring services to meet their specific needs shows a level of care that goes beyond basic customer service. This personal touch can make customers feel appreciated and more likely to remain loyal to the dealership.

Incorporating customer feedback into business operations is another way to improve service and satisfaction. Regularly soliciting feedback through surveys, comment cards, or online reviews, and then acting on that feedback, shows that the business is committed to continuous improvement based on their customers' experiences.

By prioritizing customer service and satisfaction, a used car business can differentiate itself in a competitive market. High standards of service attract and retain customers, ultimately contributing to the business's profitability and growth. In the used car market, where trust and reliability are crucial, excelling in customer service can lead to a sustainable and successful enterprise.

Record-Keeping and Administration

Effective record-keeping and administration are critical components of operations management in a used car business. These practices ensure that the business operates smoothly, remains compliant with legal standards, and is able to make informed decisions based on accurate data.

Record-keeping in a used car dealership involves maintaining detailed logs of vehicle purchases, sales, and inventory levels. Each vehicle should have a file documenting its purchase, any repairs or modifications made, its sale price, and the customer details for the sale. This not only helps in tracking the profitability of each car but also assists in managing inventory efficiently.

Financial record-keeping is equally crucial. Accurate records must be kept for all transactions, including income from car sales, expenses such as employee salaries, utility bills, and maintenance costs, and profits. These records are essential for preparing financial statements, filing taxes, and analyzing the financial health of the business. Regular financial reporting can help identify trends, such as which cars are the most profitable or what times of year yield the highest sales, aiding in strategic planning and budgeting.

Compliance with legal standards requires meticulous record-keeping. This includes documentation related to licensing, vehicle titles, warranties, and consumer contracts. Ensuring that all paperwork is correctly filled out and filed is necessary to avoid legal pitfalls and maintain the business's reputation. Regular audits of these records can help prevent potential legal issues and ensure compliance with state and federal laws.

Employee management is another area where effective administration is essential. This includes keeping accurate records of employee information, job descriptions, performance evaluations, and payroll. Properly managing this information helps in scheduling, task assignment, and evaluating employee performance, which in turn enhances overall productivity.

Customer relationship management (CRM) systems play a vital role in record-keeping by organizing customer data, sales interactions, and follow-up details. This information can be invaluable for marketing efforts, such as personalized promotions and loyalty programs, and for improving customer service by keeping track of preferences and purchase histories.

Inventory management systems are also important for a used car business. These systems help track which vehicles are in stock, which are sold, and what needs to be ordered or replenished. They can also alert the business owner to trends, like which models are selling quickly or slowly, allowing for better decision-making regarding future purchases and sales strategies.

Technology plays a crucial role in modernizing record-keeping and administration. Investing in good quality software that integrates various aspects of the business can lead to more streamlined operations. This integration can lead to improved efficiency, reduced errors, and more accessible data for making quick and informed business decisions.

In conclusion, robust record-keeping and administration are foundational to the success of a used car business. They enable effective management of finances, compliance, inventory, and human resources, all of which are necessary for sustaining and growing the business in a competitive market. With the proper systems in place, a used car dealership can operate more efficiently, be better prepared for audits, and provide excellent service to its customers.

Legal and Ethical Considerations

Compliance with Automotive Laws

Starting a used car business requires strict adherence to both state and federal automotive laws to ensure the legality and ethical operation of the enterprise. Compliance is critical not only to avoid legal repercussions but also to build trust and maintain a good reputation among customers.

Each state has its own set of regulations governing the sale of used cars. These typically include obtaining the proper licenses, such as a dealer license, which necessitates a thorough application process that may involve background checks, a bond, and proof of a physical location designed for conducting business. Ensuring that the business location complies with zoning laws is also crucial, as these regulations determine where a dealership can be located.

In addition to licensing, dealers must follow specific laws related to the sale of vehicles. One key area is the disclosure requirement, which mandates dealers to provide accurate information about the condition of the car. This includes revealing any known defects or issues that could affect the vehicle's performance or safety. The

Federal Trade Commission's Used Car Rule requires dealers to display a Buyer's Guide in every used car they offer for sale, specifying whether the vehicle is being sold "as is" or with a warranty, and what percentage of repair costs a dealer will pay under the warranty.

Title laws are also paramount. Dealers must ensure that a vehicle's title is clean and unencumbered, meaning it isn't stolen or previously salvaged unless explicitly stated. Managing title paperwork correctly is essential to avoid legal problems that can arise from title washing or failing to transfer ownership properly.

Furthermore, odometer law compliance is essential. Federal law prohibits tampering with a vehicle's odometer and requires accurate mileage reporting during the sale to prevent odometer fraud. Providing false information can lead to severe penalties, including fines and imprisonment.

Privacy regulations also play a significant role in the operation of a used car business. Dealers must protect the personal information of their customers. This involves proper handling, storage, and disposal of customer records to prevent unauthorized access or data breaches. Compliance with the Gramm-Leach-Bliley Act, which governs the collection and disclosure of customers' personal information by financial institutions, is also required for dealers offering financing options.

Environmental regulations must not be overlooked. Dealerships dealing with vehicle repair or maintenance must manage waste products according to state and federal environmental laws, including proper disposal of oil, coolant, and other hazardous materials to avoid environmental contamination.

Ethical considerations are equally important and closely tied to legal compliance. Ethical business practices involve more than just adhering to the law. They encompass fairness in advertising, transparent pricing, respectful treatment of customers and employees, and responsibility towards the community and environment. Ethical practices not only support compliance but also contribute to building a solid business reputation.

Overall, compliance with automotive laws is a complex but essential aspect of running a used car business. It ensures that dealers operate within the legal framework, providing protection to both the business and its customers. Moreover, legal and ethical compliance establishes the foundation for a successful dealership that can sustainably grow in the competitive automotive market.

Ethical Selling Practices

Ethical selling practices are crucial for the success and reputation of any used car business. These practices ensure transparency, foster trust, and promote long-term customer relationships, which are vital in an industry often stereotyped for questionable sales tactics.

One key aspect of ethical selling in the used car industry is providing full disclosure about the condition of the vehicles sold. This involves being honest about the car's history, including any accidents, repairs, and the true mileage. Dealers should provide potential buyers with vehicle history reports and maintenance records, allowing customers to make informed decisions. This transparency not only builds trust but also reduces the likelihood of post-sale disputes and legal issues.

Another important ethical practice is offering fair pricing. Prices should be set based on accurate market data and the actual condition of the car, without hidden fees or misleading cost structures. Pricing should be consistent and non-discriminatory, ensuring that all customers are treated equally. Providing clear and upfront pricing information helps to avoid confusion and builds customer confidence in the dealer's integrity.

Additionally, ethical selling involves adhering to advertising standards that avoid false or misleading claims. Advertisements should clearly represent the cars being sold, including details about the features, benefits, and limitations of the vehicle. Misleading advertisements can lead to customer dissatisfaction, damage to the business's reputation, and legal repercussions.

Customer privacy is another critical element in ethical selling practices. This means responsibly handling sensitive customer information, such as credit reports, personal details, and financial data. Dealers should have robust privacy policies in place and ensure they comply with all relevant data protection regulations to safeguard customer information from misuse or unauthorized access.

Ethical selling also encompasses fair treatment of customers. This means providing courteous service and respecting customers' rights to consider their purchase decisions without undue pressure. High-pressure sales tactics can lead to regretful buyers and a tarnished business reputation. Instead, sales personnel should be trained to assist and educate buyers, helping them find a vehicle that meets their needs and budget without coercion.

Resolving customer complaints ethically and professionally is another cornerstone of ethical selling. Effective complaint resolution procedures should be established to address any issues customers may encounter. This not only involves rectifying the immediate problem but also taking steps to prevent future occurrences. Handling complaints well can turn a potentially negative experience into a positive one, enhancing customer loyalty.

Finally, commitment to continuous improvement in ethical standards is vital. This can involve regular training for sales staff on ethical practices and legal compliance, staying updated with changes in consumer protection laws, and seeking feedback from customers to improve service quality.

Overall, integrating ethical selling practices in a used car business not only ensures compliance with legal requirements but also builds a solid foundation for customer trust and business success. These practices are essential for differentiating a business in a competitive market and achieving long-term sustainability.

Handling Legal Disputes

Handling legal disputes effectively is crucial for maintaining the integrity and longevity of a used car business. Disputes can arise in various areas including consumer complaints, contract issues, regulatory compliance, and employee relations. To manage these effectively, it's essential to establish a robust legal framework from the outset.

One key aspect is ensuring compliance with all relevant laws and regulations that govern the sale of used cars. This includes state and federal consumer protection laws, which set out the obligations of dealers to disclose certain information about the vehicles they sell, such as the car's condition, history, and any prior damages. Regular training sessions for all employees on legal requirements and ethical sales practices can prevent many potential disputes by ensuring that staff understand their obligations under the law.

Another common area of legal dispute involves warranties and guarantees. Offering clear, written explanations of what is covered by any warranty offered with vehicles can help prevent misunderstandings that might lead to disputes. It's also wise to be straightforward about the sale terms, including any return policies or satisfaction guarantees. Clear communication of these policies not only builds trust with customers but also reduces the risk of legal challenges.

When disputes do occur, having a formal dispute resolution process in place can help resolve issues before they escalate. This might include internal procedures for handling complaints and a clear method for escalating issues that cannot be resolved at the initial point of contact. For more serious disputes that involve legal claims, it may be necessary to engage the services of a lawyer who specializes in automotive or consumer law.

Documentation plays a critical role in dispute resolution. Maintaining thorough records of all transactions, communications, and interactions with customers can provide crucial evidence if disputes become formal legal challenges. This includes contracts, sales receipts, warranty information, communications about the car's condition, and any reports of issues or repairs.

For disputes involving employees, it is important to handle these with care and in accordance with employment law. Proper employee contracts, clear policies and procedures, and regular training can mitigate many common issues. Should disputes arise, they should be addressed promptly and fairly, using an established procedure that complies with employment laws to avoid further complications or legal challenges.

In addition to these measures, purchasing liability insurance can provide additional protection by covering legal fees and settlements that may arise from disputes. This kind of insurance is a worthwhile investment, protecting the business's finances and reputation in the event of significant legal issues.

Finally, fostering an ethical culture within the dealership is perhaps the most fundamental strategy for avoiding legal disputes. This involves more than just adhering to the letter of the law; it requires cultivating a commitment to fairness, honesty, and respect in every aspect of the business. An ethical approach to business not only enhances the dealership's reputation but also reduces the likelihood of disputes by building trust and goodwill with customers and the community.

Handling legal disputes in a used car business, therefore, involves a combination of proactive compliance, clear communication, thorough documentation, proper insurance coverage, and a strong ethical foundation. These elements work together to minimize the incidence of disputes and handle them effectively when they occur.

Expanding Your Business

Scaling Up Operations

Scaling up operations in a used car business involves strategic planning and execution to ensure that growth is sustainable and profitable. As the business begins to generate steady revenue and establish a solid customer base, exploring expansion opportunities becomes a viable next step.

One of the first areas to consider when scaling up is increasing the inventory. This can mean not only adding more cars but also diversifying the types of vehicles offered. For instance, incorporating luxury cars, electric vehicles, or specific high-demand models can attract a broader range of customers. To successfully expand inventory, it's crucial to have a deep understanding of market trends and customer preferences. This knowledge can be gained through market research, customer feedback, and analyzing sales data to identify which cars are selling well and which aren't.

Enhancing the physical space is another key aspect of scaling up. This might involve moving to a larger lot or acquiring additional lots in strategic locations. The choice of location can significantly impact visibility and sales, so selecting areas with high traffic volumes and good accessibility for customers is essential. Additionally, upgrading facilities to make them more appealing and comfortable for customers can enhance the buying experience and help increase sales.

Integrating technology can streamline operations and support growth. Implementing a robust inventory management system can help track vehicle information efficiently, manage costs, and optimize inventory turnover. Customer relationship management (CRM) software can also be invaluable in managing customer interactions, tracking sales processes, and marketing to potential and existing customers more effectively. Online sales platforms and digital marketing strategies are becoming increasingly important in the used car industry, allowing businesses to reach a wider audience and conduct sales beyond their immediate geographical area.

Hiring more staff and training them properly is crucial as the business expands. Adding salespeople, administrative personnel, and mechanics can ensure that the customer service quality remains high even as customer volume increases. Providing ongoing training for new and existing employees ensures that all team members are knowledgeable about the latest industry trends and sales techniques, which is vital for maintaining service quality and operational efficiency.

Exploring financing options is another component of scaling up. Growth often requires significant capital investment, whether for purchasing additional inventory, expanding facilities, or hiring staff. Securing financing through loans, investors, or reinvesting business profits can provide the necessary funds to support expansion activities.

Lastly, developing partnerships and networks can facilitate scaling up operations. Collaborating with other businesses, such as repair shops, auto parts suppliers, or financial institutions, can offer mutual benefits. These partnerships can help provide services that enhance the customer experience, extend the range of products offered, or improve business operations.

Scaling up a used car business requires careful consideration of various factors including inventory management, facility expansion, technology integration, staffing, financing, and partnerships. Each of these elements plays a crucial role in not just expanding the business, but also ensuring it thrives in a competitive market. Successful scaling ultimately depends on the ability to maintain high-quality service and customer satisfaction while managing larger operational demands.

Diversifying Inventory

Diversifying inventory is a crucial strategy for expanding a used car business and maintaining its competitiveness in the market. By offering a wider range of vehicles, a dealership can attract a broader customer base, meet varying consumer demands, and enhance its resilience against market fluctuations.

To effectively diversify inventory, a dealership should consider including different types and brands of cars. This involves stocking a mix of economy cars, luxury vehicles, SUVs, trucks, and hybrids or electric vehicles. Each category appeals to different segments of the market, from budget-conscious buyers seeking fuel-efficient compact cars to families looking for spacious SUVs or professionals in search of luxury models. By covering more market segments, a dealership not only increases its potential customer base but also mitigates risks associated with changes in consumer preferences or economic downturns that might affect one particular segment.

Incorporating specialty vehicles or those with unique features can also set a dealership apart from competitors. For example, offering cars with advanced technology features, such as autonomous driving capabilities or integrated advanced entertainment systems, can attract tech-savvy consumers. Additionally, maintaining a selection of classic or vintage cars can appeal to enthusiasts and collectors, often at higher profit margins due to their rarity and desirability.

Another aspect of inventory diversification involves the source of the vehicles. Purchasing from a variety of sources, including car auctions, trade-ins, and private sellers, can provide access to a wider range of vehicle types and conditions, allowing for a more diverse inventory. Building relationships with leasing companies or fleet operators can also be beneficial, as they often sell off vehicles in bulk, providing a steady supply of relatively new and well-maintained units.

Understanding local market trends and customer preferences is vital when diversifying inventory. Regularly reviewing sales data and customer feedback can help in identifying which types of vehicles are in high demand and which are less popular. This data-driven approach ensures that the dealership can adapt its inventory based on actual sales trends and customer needs, rather than merely speculating.

Training sales staff to be knowledgeable about a diverse inventory is equally important. Each type of vehicle has its own selling points and potential customer concerns. A well-informed sales team can effectively communicate the benefits of different types of vehicles and help customers make informed decisions based on their needs and preferences.

Marketing also plays a significant role in the successful diversification of inventory. Promoting the range of available vehicles through various channels, including online platforms, social media, and traditional advertising, helps in reaching different demographic groups. Special promotions or events can draw attention to newly added vehicle types or features, creating excitement and drawing customers to the dealership.

Lastly, maintaining financial flexibility is essential when diversifying inventory. It requires a balance between investing in new types of inventory and managing cash flow to ensure the business remains profitable and sustainable. This might involve adjusting floor plan financing or re-evaluating inventory turnover goals to accommodate the broader range of vehicles.

Diversifying inventory, when managed effectively, can lead to increased sales, higher customer satisfaction, and the overall growth of a used car business. It enables dealerships to respond dynamically to changing market conditions and customer preferences, thereby securing a competitive edge in the automotive industry.

Franchising Opportunities

Franchising is an excellent way to expand a used car business, allowing entrepreneurs to grow their brand while minimizing the risks and capital typically required for expansion. By adopting a franchise model, used car business owners can leverage their successful business formula and replicate it in new markets through partnerships with franchisees.

Franchising offers a structured approach to business expansion where the franchisor provides the franchisee with all the necessary tools, systems, and processes to operate under the established brand name. This includes branding materials, operational procedures, software, training programs, and ongoing support. In return, the franchisee pays initial franchise fees and ongoing royalties, which are usually based on a percentage of their revenue.

The benefit of this model is that it taps into the local knowledge and capital of the franchisees. Since franchisees are typically from the local area in which they operate, they bring valuable insights into the local market, consumer behavior, and potentially beneficial business connections. This local expertise can be critical in adapting the business model to suit regional preferences and regulations, which might be difficult for a centralized owner to manage effectively.

Moreover, franchising can lead to rapid brand expansion. With multiple franchisees operating in different regions, the brand can quickly gain national recognition and a broader customer base. This widespread brand presence not only drives more business to individual franchises but also enhances the brand's overall market strength against competitors.

Financially, franchising is attractive because it reduces the burden of capital expenditure and operational costs on the franchisor. Since franchisees finance their own startup and operational costs, the franchisor's financial risks are significantly reduced. This setup also motivates franchisees to perform well since they have a direct stake in the business's success.

For the used car business, franchising also allows for diversification of inventory and services. Franchisees might bring in vehicles unique to their local markets or demand different types of services, such as specific financing options or after-sales support. This diversification can enrich the entire franchise network by sharing what works across different locations, potentially leading to innovations in sales tactics, marketing strategies, and customer service practices.

However, franchising also requires careful management and a strong support system to ensure quality and consistency across all locations. The franchisor must establish comprehensive training programs to ensure that franchisees and their staff understand the business model, company culture, and expected service standards. Regular audits and visits to franchise locations can help maintain these standards.

Setting up a franchising system involves legal considerations as well, including drafting detailed franchise agreements and complying with local and national franchising laws. These legal documents must clearly define the relationship between the franchisor and the franchisee, including the rights and responsibilities of each party, to avoid conflicts and ensure smooth operations.

In essence, while franchising can provide a powerful path for expansion, it requires a commitment to support and maintain high standards throughout the network. For entrepreneurs with a successful used car business, franchising offers a pathway to leverage their business model, expand their brand, and generate substantial growth through collaborative partnerships.

Partnerships and Alliances

Expanding a used car business through partnerships and alliances is a strategic move that can lead to substantial growth and diversification. Forming partnerships with other businesses within the automotive industry or related fields can open up new revenue streams, enhance the business's service offerings, and provide access to new customer bases.

One effective approach is partnering with auto repair shops or service centers. This type of alliance allows a used car dealership to offer complimentary services such as maintenance and repairs, which can be a strong selling point for customers. It also provides the repair shops with a steady flow of customers, creating a mutually beneficial relationship. This partnership can be formalized through co-marketing efforts, shared space agreements, or referral incentives, ensuring both parties benefit from increased traffic and business.

Another valuable partnership can be formed with auto parts suppliers. This connection ensures that the dealership maintains a consistent and cost-effective supply of parts necessary for vehicle reconditioning, which is crucial for maintaining the quality and appeal of the inventory. In return, suppliers gain a reliable buyer for their products, which could lead to negotiated discounts or exclusive deals, further reducing costs and improving profit margins for the dealership.

Financial institutions play a crucial role in the expansion of a used car business. Establishing strong relationships with banks and finance companies can help facilitate the financing options available to customers, making it easier for them to purchase vehicles. This not only enhances the customer experience by providing flexible payment options but also increases sales conversions by broadening the pool of potential buyers.

Technology partnerships can also be transformative, especially in today's digital age. Collaborating with software providers or online platforms can enhance the dealership's online presence and sales capabilities. For example, integrating inventory management systems, CRM software, and digital marketing tools can streamline operations and improve customer engagement. Additionally, partnerships with online car listing sites or e-commerce platforms can expand the dealership's reach, allowing it to tap into a larger market.

Collaborations with local businesses and community organizations can also be beneficial. These alliances help in building the dealership's reputation and visibility in the community through joint promotional events, sponsorships, or charity drives. Such community engagement not only fosters good will but also attracts local customers who prefer to support businesses that contribute positively to their community.

Lastly, considering strategic alliances with rental car agencies or corporate fleets can provide a steady source of well-maintained used cars and open up opportunities for bulk purchases and sales. These vehicles, often sold off by such entities to renew their fleets, can be acquired at competitive prices and sold with a history of regular maintenance and professional use, appealing to a segment of buyers interested in reliability and comprehensive service records.

In summary, expanding a used car business through partnerships and alliances offers numerous benefits, including enhanced service offerings, access to new markets, cost efficiencies, and improved customer satisfaction. By carefully selecting partners that align with the dealership's goals and customer needs, a used car business can significantly enhance its market position and achieve sustainable growth.

Challenges and Solutions

Common Pitfalls and How to Avoid Them

Starting a used car business comes with its set of challenges, and being aware of these pitfalls can help entrepreneurs navigate through them successfully. One of the most common pitfalls is poor location choice. A location that lacks visibility or accessibility can significantly reduce customer foot traffic, limiting sales opportunities. To avoid this, thorough market research should be conducted to identify high-traffic areas that are easily accessible and visible. Choosing a location near major roadways or commercial hubs can enhance visibility and attract more customers.

Another frequent issue is inadequate inventory management. Holding too much inventory can tie up capital, while too little can lead to lost sales. Effective inventory management involves understanding market demand and maintaining a diverse range of vehicles that appeal to different customer preferences and budgets. Regularly reviewing sales data and market trends helps adjust inventory to meet customer needs dynamically.

Pricing strategy errors can also derail a used car business. Setting prices too high can drive away potential buyers, while pricing too low can erode profits. Competitive pricing is crucial and can be achieved by researching local market prices and adjusting accordingly to offer value while maintaining a healthy profit margin.

Financing issues are another major challenge. Used car buyers often require financing options, and not offering these can limit sales. Establishing relationships with financial institutions and offering flexible financing options can help attract a broader customer base. Additionally, managing the business's finances poorly can lead to cash flow problems. Regular financial analysis and budgeting are essential to ensure the business remains profitable and financially healthy.

Legal compliance is also critical. The used car industry is highly regulated, and failing to comply with local, state, and federal regulations can result in hefty fines and legal challenges. Dealers must stay informed about the latest regulations in the automotive industry, including consumer protection laws and environmental regulations regarding vehicle emissions.

Marketing missteps can prevent a used car business from reaching its full potential. An ineffective marketing strategy may fail to attract the right customers. Investing in a strong online presence, leveraging social media, and employing targeted advertising can improve visibility and attract more customers. Additionally, building a good reputation through excellent customer service and trustworthy business practices encourages word-of-mouth referrals and repeat business.

Lastly, neglecting customer experience can have detrimental effects on sales and business growth. In today's competitive market, customers expect not only a good product but also exceptional service. Providing excellent customer service, being transparent about car histories, and ensuring the sales process is customer-friendly are all crucial for fostering customer loyalty and enhancing business reputation.

By being aware of these challenges and strategically addressing them, entrepreneurs can significantly increase their chances of success in the used car industry.

Handling Economic Downturns

Handling economic downturns is a significant challenge for any business, especially in industries sensitive to consumer spending like the used car market. However, with strategic planning and adaptability, a used car business can not only survive but potentially thrive during these periods.

During economic downturns, consumers typically tighten their budgets, which can reduce the frequency and volume of car purchases. However, the demand for used cars often remains more stable or even increases compared to new cars because they are more affordable. Understanding this trend, used car dealers can adjust their inventory to include more budget-friendly, fuel-efficient, and reliable vehicles that appeal to cost-conscious buyers.

Cash flow management becomes crucial in downturns. Keeping overheads low and managing inventory without overextending financially is vital. This may involve more stringent checks on which cars to buy for resale, focusing on those that require minimal reconditioning to turn a profit. Implementing a rigorous budget and cutting non-essential expenses can help maintain a healthy cash flow.